crawl,

play

push

carry

hold

snuggle

The
Baby
Book

Published by Silver Press,
A Division of Simon & Schuster
299 Jefferson Road, Parsippany, New Jersey 07054

Designed by Studio Goodwin Sturges

Manufactured in the United States of America
10 9 8 7 6 5 4 3 2 1

Library of Congress Cataloging-in-Publication Data

Morris, Ann, 1930-
The baby book / by Ann Morris: photographs by Ken Heyman.
p. cm.—(The World's Family series)
Summary: Photographs of babies from many nations,
engaged in typical activities.
1. Infants—Juvenile literature. I. Heyman, Ken, ill.
II. Title. III. Series.
HQ774.M64 1996
305.23'2—dc20   95-14261   CIP   AC
ISBN 0-382-24698-5 (JHC) ISBN 0-382-24699-3 (LSB)
ISBN 0-382-24700-0 (PBK)

The Baby Book

By Ann Morris
Photographs by Ken Heyman

Silver Press
Parsippany, New Jersey

Everyone loves babies!

Here's what babies do.

Babies eat.

They are always hungry.

Babies sleep

and sleep

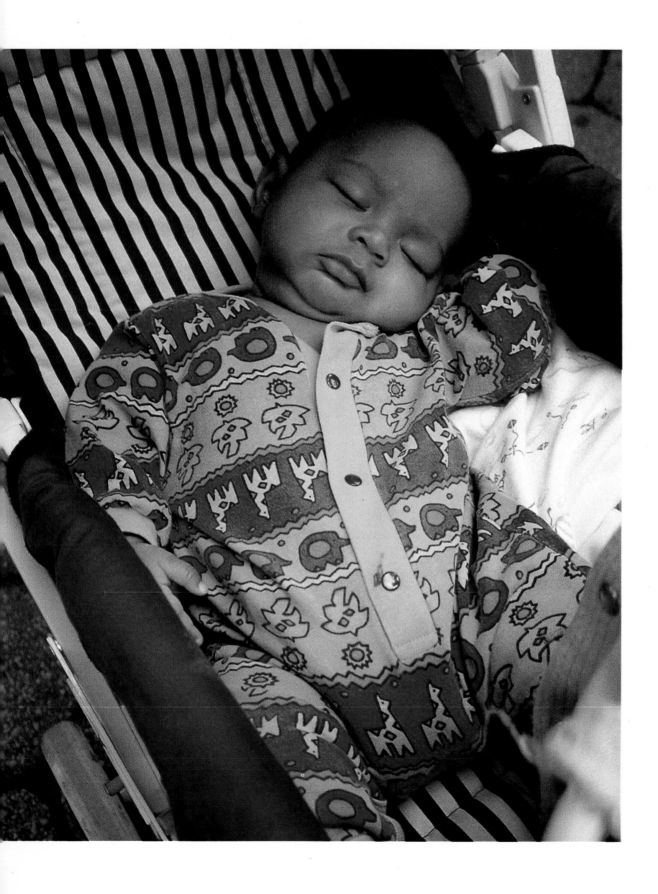

and cuddle

and snuggle.

Babies splash in the bath.

Babies crawl.

Babies are happy,

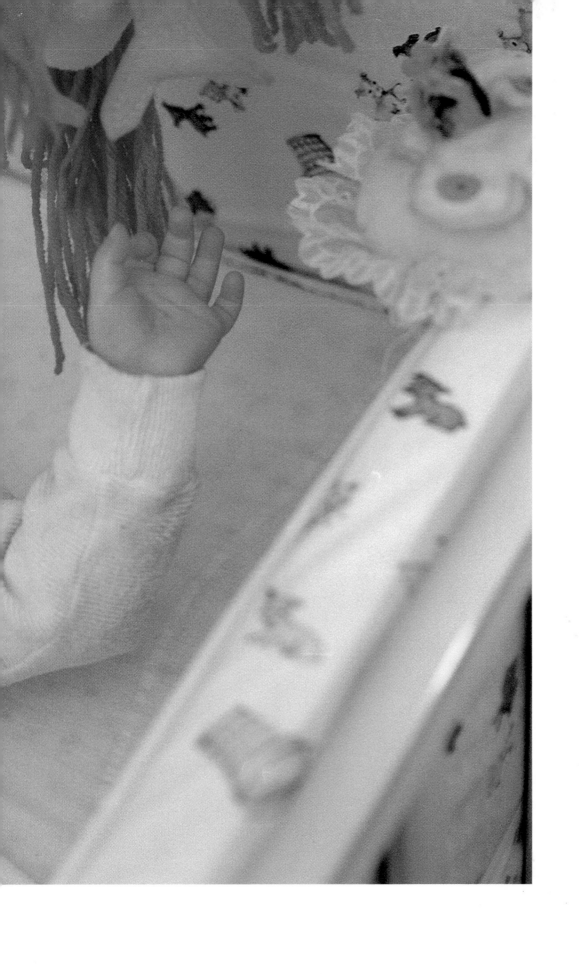

sad,

and curious.

They like to make friends.

Babies play every day.

They are carried

and pushed

and held up high.

Everybody loves babies!

Index to the Babies

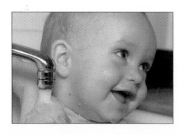

Page 17: The twins are learning to crawl.

Page 18: Jason is very happy in his crib, surrounded by safe cushions.

Page 20: In Brazil, this older sister watches her brother while her mother works.

Page 21: In Guatemala, this little baby is carried in an all-purpose blanket that warms and protects her.

Page 22: The older child tries to deliver a telephone message to the younger child.

Page 23: This Navajo father becomes friends with his daughter in their hogan, a round Navajo house with one room.

Page 24: Sometimes it seems that a baby just plays and plays.

Page 25: This Japanese American child learns through playing with his toys.

Page 26: The mother in the Samburu tribe of Kenya carries her baby close to her.

Page 27: These twins in New York City are seeing all the sights.

Page 28: Babies love to be held high, especially by their daddies.

Page 29: New baby brothers and sisters are very special.

Ann Morris

Ann Morris's many books for children include **Bread Bread Bread, Hats Hats Hats, How Teddy Bears Are Made** and **Dancing to America**. She has been a teacher in public and private schools and has taught courses in language arts, children's literature, and writing for children at Bank Street College, Teachers College, Queens College of the City University of New York, and at The New School in New York City.

Ken Heyman

Ken Heyman's photographic career has taken him into the heart of many indigenous cultures. His photographs have appeared in publications such as **Life, Look,** and **The New York Times**, and his work has been exhibited on three continents. His photographs illustrate numerous children's books, and he is the co-author of **Family** with Margaret Mead. He lives in New York City.

eat

sleep

do

cuddle

love

splash